MW00476785

Montessori at Home Guide

GENTLE PARENTING TECHNIQUES TO
HELP YOUR 2 TO 6-YEAR-OLD LEARN
SOCIAL SKILLS AND DISCIPLINE

Rachel Peachey

Sterling Production
LEXINGTON, KENTUCKY

Sterling Production
www.sterlingproduction.com
ashleyandmitch@sterlingproduction.com

Montessori at Home Guide: Gentle Parenting Techniques to Help your 2 to 6-Year-Old Learn Social Skills and Discipline
Rachel Peachey
ISBN-13: 9781521004067

Table of Contents

To my parents, who have always supported me and taught me the importance of dialogue and conflict resolution.

"Discipline is, therefore, primarily a learning experience"
- DR. MARIA MONTESSORI

CHAPTER ONE

Introduction

Parenting is the most difficult and rewarding job most parents will ever have. The emotions, joys and challenges that are faced during this journey are unmatched by anything else in life. The moment your precious baby is born, love, concern and a fierce instinct to protect your little one also arise.

As our children grow, so do the challenges as we attempt to guide and mold them into good people who are kind, caring and well-adapted. In addition, we also want to ensure we give them the tools necessary to succeed in life and be happy. To achieve these goals, most parents teach social skills and use discipline within the home.

Dr. Maria Montessori offers some helpful thoughts, techniques and insights regarding how parents and teachers can approach discipline and social skills with children.

Before continuing to introduce Montessori herself, I think it's important to note that one of Montessori's key principles is to follow the child. By observing our children carefully, we can discover all of their needs and interests. So, when considering teaching social skills and discipline with our children, we must keep in mind that our methods must be developmentally appropriate. In this book, we're focusing on children ages 2-6.

During this exciting time, children change drastically. At two, children, although growing in their independence, are still unstable physically. They may totter and struggle to use their pudgy hands to perform tasks requiring fine motor skills. They can express themselves to a point, but most are still quite limited in their communication. By six, children are very independent and communicative. They can run, jump and climb skillfully and narrate full stories.

Throughout these years, children are naturally driven to learn to do things on their own and develop their motor and language skills. They are curious and many even go through a stage of asking "why?" about everything.

In their push for independence, they also clash with their parents and caregivers. They explore limits and express their emotions fully, sometimes lashing out and becoming violent. Frustration and disappointment are ever present as children struggle between what they can and can't do on their own. Children also slowly become more and more aware of others, their feelings and what is considered appropriate and inappropriate behavior.

This book addresses the Montessori perspective on teaching social skills and discipline. The word discipline is used because this is the most popular, easily understood word to refer to guiding a child's behavior. In this context, discipline is used to refer to setting limits and working with children regarding expectations and guiding towards appropriate behavior.

However, in Montessori, challenges and key triggers for children are also avoided by creating a space that's friendly and open for them. Many common discipline issues can be prevented simply by meeting some of the child's basic needs, which between the ages of 2-6 includes independence, freedom, choice, stimulating and interesting activities, opportunities for movement and socializing among others.

Montessori had a scientific way of approaching children and learning. Perhaps it was her scientific background from going to medical school that led her to study children and development in this way.

Montessori, who graduated as a trained doctor in 1896, looked at children and their growth in a whole new way that is considered revolutionary even today!

As part of her scientific approach to studying and working with children, Montessori followed some of the typical traditional ways of interacting with children to see how it worked. For example, she used rewards and punishments in the classroom and was surprised to find that this wasn't the best way. In her words:

"And I was astonished when I learned that a child who is permitted to educate himself really gives up these lower instincts.

I then urged the teachers to cease handing out the ordinary prizes and punishments, which were no longer suited to our children, and to confine themselves to directing them gently in their work."

In her work developing a new methodology for teaching children, she discovered many more effective ways for guiding children to be helpful, positive members within their communities. It is these techniques, ideas and principles that will be expanded upon in this book. I hope you will be inspired and encouraged by the practical suggestions and food for thought discussed in this book as you continue your parenting journey.

"What is social life if not the solving of social problems, behaving properly and pursuing aims acceptable to all? [It is not] sitting side by side and hearing someone else talk..."
- DR. MARIA MONTESSORI

CHAPTER TWO

Basic Social Skills

"Miss Rachel, they won't let me play!" I turned around to find a distraught 4-year-old girl tugging at my sleeve. It was outdoor play time and children were enjoying the fresh air, busily playing "house".

I crouched down beside her. "Well, did you try asking them if you can play?" I asked.

"No," she said thoughtfully.

"Do you want to go ask?" I said.

"Ok," she said and ran off.

I observed as the girl approached the group of children. I saw how they quickly decided on a role for her to play in the house and continued in their game.

A simple social skill, such as asking to join a group in this case, can make the difference between feeling left out and helpless, and feeling included, happy and at peace. With support and guidance, children can learn social skills to help them navigate the many interactions with others in daily life.

Montessori believed that a truly respectful, polite community could be created among children. In order to achieve this harmonious environment, Montessori believed in taking the time to teach social skills intentionally to children. In many Montessori schools, these lessons are known as the "grace and courtesy" lessons.

Lessons in grace and courtesy teach children the appropriate and socially acceptable ways of dealing with common situations. In the classroom, these skills are often taught to the whole class during circle time or may be taught to smaller groups of students. As parents, you can teach these skills one on one to your child, although in some cases, it's ideal to have a few more people or children around. Even the most basic social skills are taught, because although these skills may seem obvious and easy to adults, it's not always the case for children. By highlighting the skill and giving children examples and practical steps to take, we can set them up for success and give them confidence when interacting with others. The social skills that will be covered in this chapter are listed below:

- Saying "Hello"
- Introducing oneself
- Introducing someone else
- Welcoming a visitor
- Inviting someone to play
- Asking to join a group
- Answering and talking on the phone
- How to interrupt politely
- Recognizing emotions in others
- Talking about feelings

In addition to using the lessons that are outlined in this chapter, it's also important to model and review these skills. As parents, we are the main examples for our children. They watch our every move. So, we must be sure that we model the skills that we are teaching in our everyday interactions.

It's also helpful to remind children about the skills just before they enter a situation in which it's likely they can make use of them. For example, if you're going to a family gathering, a play date, or a party, remind your child how to say hello and introduce themselves. With more and more practice, your child will be able to identify situations in which each of the skills learned are appropriate.

Some children are naturals at these skills and excel at interacting with others. Other children are more reserved and may need more support as they initiate interactions with other children. You can offer to hold their hand, stand beside them or say "hello" as well, especially when meeting someone new. With time, even the most reserved children will gain the confidence to begin to make use of social skills on their own. As a teacher, I've also noticed that when parents *aren't* around, children may also become braver and more confident when using social skills and interacting with other children. So, if you think your child is a bit shy or reserved, don't sweat it. With patience, encouragement, and practice, your child will slowly be able to use many of these skills on their own.

Please note that these activities are written assuming you'll be doing the lessons in a one on one situation unless the activity is best suited for a group. If you choose to do the lesson with a group, adjust to include all children in any discussions and role-playing.

Saying "Hello"

Ideally for this presentation a small group of children should be present and sitting in a circle. Then, explain that when we see a friend who we already know or see someone new, that we can greet them by saying "hello". Also, explain to the children that you can shake hands as a greeting. Demonstrate with another child how to shake hands.

Then, ask the children to take turns saying "hello" and shaking hands around the circle, with each person greeting the person on their right. You can repeat the exercise having the children give a high five or a hug if they want.

Songs can also be helpful for teaching how to greet one another. You can also include a "hello" song as an addition to the lesson. A quick search on Youtube.com will bring up many appropriate songs you can teach to children. It's best to learn the song yourself, and then teach it to the children. If you choose to allow the children to hear the song, it's best done without the video so that they can focus on the words and the music. Then, practice singing the "hello" song together.

As an extension, you can have children add on "How are you?" to their greeting. This is best done after you've taken some time to talk about emotions and feelings. There's a lesson in this chapter that discusses feelings for reference. Once children are comfortable naming emotions, ask them to greet each other around the circle saying "Hello, how are you?" to the person on their right and responding.

Introducing Oneself

This lesson can be done with a small group or one on one. So, if you have several children, you can do it with them together, or just with one of them.

Explain to your child that when you meet someone you don't know, it's polite to introduce yourself. Then tell your child that you are going to demonstrate how to introduce yourself. Ask your child to imagine that you don't know each other. Then, proceed to introduce yourself, saying "Hi, my name is _____. What's your name?" Next, ask your child to try introducing themselves.

Take time to review this lesson prior to situations in which your child is likely to meet someone new.

Introducing Someone Else

This lesson can be done with a small group or one on one. If you choose to do it one on one, it will involve pretending that someone else is there.

Start by explaining to your child that sometimes two friends might not know each other. Try to give a real-life example so they can understand. Then tell your child that you will demonstrate how you might introduce a friend to someone else.

You can say something like "Sarah, this is my friend Dan. Dan, this is my friend Sarah."

Then ask your child to try.

Take time to review this lesson prior to situations in which your child is likely to have a need to introduce someone else. For example, if your child has a party or takes a friend along with them to an event or activity.

Welcoming A Visitor

This lesson can be done as a one on one or in a group.

Explain to your child that you're going to talk about welcoming a visitor. Depending on the age of your child, you may want to discuss what a visitor is and if they remember having any visitors at their house or school. Also, ask if they've ever been a visitor and what it's like. Mention that as a visitor, they may feel uncertain or nervous.

Then proceed to explain that to help visitors feel more welcome, it's nice to greet and welcome a visitor. Explain that you're going to demonstrate greeting and welcoming a visitor. You may have your child pretend to be the visitor. Say something like:

"Hi, welcome to our house! I'm so glad you're here." Then ask your child to try.

As an extension, you can come up with a list of things that the visitor might like or need to know upon arriving. For example:

- A cup of water
- A cup of tea or coffee (for adults during colder seasons)
- Where the bathroom is
- To hang up their coat or jacket
- A place to sit

After you've made your list, you can practice role playing and offering these things to the visitor.

Inviting Someone to Play

This can be a one on one or group lesson.

Ask your child if they've ever watched other children playing and wished they could join. Take the time to talk about how it feels to want to join, but be too scared to ask or to not know the kids who are playing. Then, discuss how that they may be playing in a group and that there may be another child who'd like to play. Make a list of ways to notice if another child might want to play. For example:

- The child is watching them play
- The child isn't playing with anyone else
- The child is sitting alone
- The child tries to join

Explain that it's nice to include the other child by inviting them to play. Demonstrate how you might ask, saying "Would you like to play with us?"

Have your child try. Then, review how to introduce oneself and how to introduce others.

Finally, discuss any next steps that must be taken. For example, if they're playing "tag" tell the newcomer who's "it", etc.

Asking to Join a Group

This lesson works well as a one on one or group lesson.

In a similar way to the lesson "Inviting Someone to Play", discuss times when they might see another group of children playing. Explain that there's an easy and polite way to join in the fun. Demonstrate asking to join, by saying "Can I please play too?" Practice role-playing with your child, switching roles.

Then, review the lesson on introducing oneself.

Answering and Talking on the Phone

This lesson works well for a group or one on one.

For this lesson, use the phone most commonly used in your home to demonstrate and practice. Explain to your child that sometimes the phone may ring and you may be unable to answer it. Tell your child that they can help you by answering the phone. If you prefer that your child only answers the phone when you ask them to, make sure that this is clear.

Tell your child that you're going to demonstrate what to say when answering the phone. For example, "Hello, this is (name)." Ask your child to try.

Then, take the conversation further by using some scenarios. For example, if you're unavailable because you're in the bathroom, tell your child they can say "I'm sorry, (name) can't come to the phone right now. May I ask who's calling?"

Or "I'm sorry, (name) can't come to the phone right now. Can I have him/her call you back?" if the name's been given.

Practice role playing a few times until your child is comfortable answering and talking on the phone.

How to Interrupt Politely

Children sometimes have a habit of interrupting their parents at inopportune times. For example, when a parent is on the phone or having an important conversation, a child may want to show their parent something.

Explain to your child that there are times when it's not ok to talk to you and that they must wait until you're finished with what you're doing before they can talk to you again. Discuss what these situations are. You may mention talking on the phone, talking with another adult or any other situations you feel are appropriate.

Then, tell your child that sometimes there are things that your child must tell you right away and that it's ok to interrupt you with. For example, if your child needs help using the bathroom, hurts themselves or simply needs to tell you something important, it may be ok to interrupt. Try to think of specific examples to help your child understand.

Explain that you're going to show your child how to interrupt politely. Demonstrate how to rest your hand on their arm and say "Excuse me, I need to tell you something."

Have your child try. Then role-play the situation, showing how you would respond to your child. You may review this lesson as necessary.

Recognizing Emotions in Others

Young children are still learning to understand feelings and recognize them in others. To increase their empathy and ability to understand others, it can be helpful to talk about feelings directly. By talking about emotions, children will learn to gauge their interactions and determine whether their actions are creating positive or negative emotions in others. Slowly, they'll show more empathy and interest in how others are feeling. This helps them build healthy interactions and relationships.

For this lesson, you'll need to do some preparation. Find real photographs of people and children showing different emotions and print them off on separate cards. Start with some basic ones, such as angry, happy, sad and surprised. As an extension, you can present the lesson again with more complex expressions such as worry, fear, confusion, excited, etc.

Tell your child that you're going to talk about feelings. Explain that people often show how they feel by making different facial expressions. Show one of the cards. Ask your child to identify the emotion. Talk about times when your child feels this way. Then, continue with the rest in the same way.

This is fine for the first lesson. Then, as a review or extension, you can watch people in a park or other public space. Notice any facial expressions and emotions that you see.

Finally, take the time to talk about each of the emotions and how it might change your interaction with others. For example, if you see that someone is angry, what might you do or say? You can practice role-plays and make lists of appropriate responses for each emotion such as "You look angry, do you want to tell me why?"

Talking about Feelings

For this lesson, ensure that you've already done the previous lesson "Recognizing Emotions in Others". You may use the same cards you had for this previous lesson as conversation starters.

Use an "emotions journal" or a sheet of paper for each emotion and pick one to start with. "Happy" is an easy one to start with. Tell your child that you're going to talk about feelings. Show them the emotion card you've chosen. Ask them about when they feel this emotion. Help your child write (or have them write if able) a list of times when they feel that emotion.

Then, ask them how they might communicate their feelings to others. Role play several situations about each emotion. For example, when talking about "angry" your child might say they feel angry when they want to use a toy that another child has. Come up with a list of some options for what your child can say together. For example: "I feel angry because I want to play with that toy" or "I'm angry because I don't want to wait for the toy."

Follow your child's interest level. Going through just one emotion for a lesson is fine. You can continue with the other emotions another day.

Review these lessons as necessary and try to help your child talk about emotions in real life as situations arise.

"...if he shows a tendency to misbehave, she will check him with earnest words..."

\- DR. MARIA MONTESSORI

CHAPTER THREE

A Montessori Approach to Discipline

"Some of these kids probably shouldn't be in this circle time anyway. They're clearly not interested in the topic," an experienced Montessori teacher said.

We had just finished a lesson with five and six-year-old's, and a few of them had been quite rowdy. It was my first year on the job and I still hadn't undergone formal Montessori training.

Her words startled me a bit. "Shouldn't be in the lesson?" I thought, "but then how will they learn the content?" I wondered to myself.

The teacher went on to suggest other work the rowdier children could do, explaining that they seemed to show a need to move around and be more active.

This moment opened my mind to one of the most basic concepts in the Montessori approach to discipline. That concept is "following the child." When children are misbehaving in our eyes, they are often communicating something that's not working in their environment.

While of course there are rules and limits that children must follow within a Montessori classroom or home, parents and teachers must also constantly evaluate the environment to ensure that the child's needs are being met. This includes thinking hard about what activities your child can handle and when. This doesn't mean that you structure your whole life around your child and don't ask your child to help with chores because they won't want to, it just means that you take the time to adjust your expectations and look at your child's behavior with new eyes.

For example, make sure your child has had a snack before you go grocery shopping to avoid meltdowns due to hunger. Or, ensure that your child has a way to exercise every day, even if it's cold in the winter where you live. Set up some indoor exercise or active space to use every day.

These are just a few examples. The idea of following your child will be a theme throughout this chapter as we look at helpful Montessori discipline techniques and some further scenarios for dealing with difficult behaviors.

Three Levels of Obedience

Since we're talking about discipline, it's important to take a minute to consider developmental milestones. Being obedient doesn't come instantaneously for children. As children grow, Montessori suggests in *The Absorbent Mind*, they develop their will. Some adults may see this as a negative, believing that a strong-willed child will produce disorder and trouble. However, Montessori urges us to consider the fact that a child's will lead them "to make progress and to develop his powers."

Her observations continue to help us understand the child's progress in developing obedience. At first, very young children (under the age of three), typically only obey when what we request happens to correspond with what they want to do in the first place. For example, you call your 2-year-old to eat lunch. If your child is hungry or enjoys the activity of eating lunch, they'll join you, showing a form of obedience. However, if your child doesn't happen to want to eat lunch, you may have to convince them or impose your will upon them. This is the first stage of obedience.

In this first stage or level of obedience, the child is inconsistent. Sometimes your child may obey, and sometimes they don't. Montessori likens it to learning to walk. Until children become proficient at walking after much practice, they sometimes fail and sometimes succeed. The same is true for being obedient. It's a skill to be learned now in their life.

The second level of obedience requires greater understanding from the child. In this level, the child understands what someone else wishes for them to do, and does it to please them. This is where most of us parents think, "Success! I ask my child to do something and they actually listen!" This is an important milestone usually reached somewhere around the age of three in which the child is obedient quite consistently, although certainly not all the time.

Montessori went further and discovered that a third level of obedience is possible. In this level, the child obeys joyfully. Basically, this means that the child sees the value in what they're being asked to do, and so completes the request because of it.

This should be our goal. Guiding our children to reaching the third level of obedience gives them the opportunity to work joyfully. On the other hand, it gives us great responsibility in making our requests.

Expectations

When children arrive to a Montessori classroom for the first time, they are invited to learn some of the basic routines used in the classroom, such as putting materials away after using them, putting out a carpet and rolling it up. Children also learn how to get the attention of the teacher, learn to watch others while they're working without disturbing them, how to pull out a chair and sit on it, and many other lessons.

What does this have to do with your home?

These lessons are taught intentionally. Children are shown a few lessons each day. The teacher patiently shows each of the steps and gives the children a chance to try.

With our children, we must go through a similar process. Our children learn many routines just by observing us and living everyday life with us. For example, most children quickly learn to flush the toilet and wash their hands after using the bathroom. Why? Because during potty learning we try for them to make this habit. We repeat it. We remind them and show them repeatedly.

Sometimes in the home we may have other expectations that we haven't made clear to our children. These typically bring frustration out for us as parents, and may also be difficult for our children as well. If we haven't made our expectations clear, it's hard for our children to follow the rules. Sometimes by taking a step back we can determine whether we've truly made our expectations clear and easy for our children to follow.

For example, some parents may wish their child picked up their toys each evening. You can make this an expectation by taking time every day to show your child how to perform this task and repeating it until it becomes habit.

Recently, I realized I was becoming frustrated that my child was leaving his dirty plate on the table. "He even washes the dishes with me quite frequently, why doesn't he take his plate to the sink?" I wondered. But on second thought, I discovered that I had never shown him otherwise! So, I showed him after a meal how to take his plate to the sink. I said "Every time you have a dirty dish, it goes here in the sink." Now he readily takes his dishes to the sink.

A quick evaluation of behaviors and habits that are frustrating can quickly help you determine whether you have properly taught the expectation. If you have taught the expectation, then you may want to use one of the techniques outlined in this chapter. If not, take the time to teach your child what the expectations and rules are.

When teaching an expectation, use these helpful guidelines:

1. Make it Special –

While you can go about teaching expectations in your everyday life, it shouldn't be done on the fly. You must be present with your child, not rattling off instructions while thumbing through your phone or looking for your keys. Life is busy for families. But, if you don't have the time to devote to your child while you teach the expectation, wait until you do.

Tell your child "I'm going to show you something new" or similar. Smile at them and ensure you have their full attention before you continue.

2. Demonstrate

The most important part of communicating your expectation is modeling it. It's more important than your words (unless you are teaching words to use!). Demonstrate exactly what you want your child to do. Then, say "Now can you try?"

3. Stay Positive

If you're frustrated with a behavior, take a deep breath before addressing it. If the expectation hasn't been taught, it's really not your child's fault. Use positive language. For example, when talking to my son about his plate, I said "Now when you're finished eating, take your plate to the sink." I didn't say "Don't leave your plate on the table." By focusing on the behavior and actions you want to see, your child will do the same.

Creating Expectations Around Your Child's Needs

Expectations must also be analyzed from a different perspective. Sometimes we have unreasonable expectations that prevent our children from meeting basic needs. The way we interact with our children can stifle the most basic instincts that guide our children's actions. Furthermore, even how we arrange our homes can affect how well we meet our children's needs.

One of the main needs of children ages 2-6 is gaining independence. Montessori very aptly sums it up: *"These very children reveal to us the most vital need of their development, saying: 'Help me to do it alone!'"*

What does this mean for our expectations?

1. Expect our children to want to be independent.

Simply by expecting our children to want to be independent, we change our mindset and perspective of our children. Many so-called discipline problems can be avoided by understanding that many of your child's actions are simply their attempt at independence. We can't expect our child to obey our every command when sometimes this acts in direct contrast with their inner teacher, who pushes them towards independence.

For example, the first instinctual reaction I had when my 18-month-old daughter tugged at me and tried to pull herself up on a tall stool to reach the counter when I was mixing up a cake, was to scoop her up so she could see. She was not happy about this. She wanted to stand on her own to see, so I ended up saying "no, this stool is too high," and put her back down on the floor (even after studying the Montessori philosophy, some of our most basic parenting reactions can be rather unhelpful). She cried. Upon reconsidering things, her only desire was to participate in this exciting activity independently. I pulled over a smaller table she could easily reach and came down to her level so that she could see, and help me stir. This story could have easily ended in a full-blown temper tantrum. But, by changing my perspective and recognizing the great desire my child had to participate independently, I avoided a potential discipline problem and my daughter was able to help stir up cake batter.

2. Encourage independence wherever possible.

This is the direct result of expecting our children to be independent. If we expect them to want to be independent, the next logical move is to encourage this independence to grow and flourish! There are many ways to do this.

First of all, you must make your home child-friendly so that your child can complete tasks independently. This may mean putting step stools around your home so that your child can reach the sink in the bathroom and counters or sinks in the kitchen. This also means making some simple snacks available for your child to access whenever they need them. In addition, art supplies should be easily accessible to your child so that they may practice. These are simple steps towards encouraging your child's independence that also help you show your child that you trust them. This will go a long way in strengthening your relationship.

One helpful way to determine whether your home is friendly to your child is to spend time on your child's level. While we parents may often find ourselves on the floor playing, we don't always truly put ourselves in their shoes. During a quiet moment, sit in different areas of your home and imagine that you are your child. Notice how high up the table is and whether or not you could reach your jacket and clothes or get a cup to drink from. By spending a bit of time doing this in each room of your house, you can ensure that your home is independence-friendly.

3. Let go of some of the control.

Our instinct is often to protect our children, sometimes to the point of preventing them from reaching their full potential. Young children need not only independence, but space and our vote of confidence in their abilities. It can be so hard not to sweep in and help our child finish a task quickly, such as carrying a heavy pitcher of water or tying their shoes. We may be worried they'll make a mistake or be in a hurry. But, only by allowing them to spill the water will they gain the skills to carry the pitcher more carefully. And only by practicing tying shoes themselves will they eventually be able to do it successfully (and quickly) on their own. So, we must let go of some of the control and allow our children to try, experiment, fail and succeed.

In addition to helping our children in meeting their most vital developmental need, discipline problems can often be avoided by changing our perspective and remembering that our children aim to be independent. How? Let's consider a few scenarios:

- Your child nags you on a regular basis that they're hungry. You've become frustrated with the whining and complaining. Even though you've tried to encourage your child to ask nicely for a snack, it's a constant battle because your child also often becomes cranky when they're hungry. Consider providing snacks for your child to prepare independently. Perhaps you can leave out a basket of fruit or a box of healthy crackers. Show your child how to prepare a snack for themselves. Then, always keep the snacks replenished. Discipline problem eliminated! Rather than becoming cranky and whining to you for a snack, your child independently prepares one whenever they're hungry. You still have the control you need as the parent because you choose the snack options.

- You got into a battle of wills with your 5-year-old about putting on clothes to go to school in the morning. You've laid out the clothes for your child, but she doesn't want to get dressed and you can't figure out why. Independence may be at play here. Rather than picking out clothes for your child, give them a few choices or allow them to pick out their outfit on their own. If needed, you can spend some time another day discussing how the weather influences what clothes are appropriate to wear.

- You are constantly saying "no" to your child and it often causes a meltdown. Whether or not you use the word "no" to communicate is irrelevant in these cases. Your child may feel as though their desire for independence is being squashed. Try to look carefully at what your child wants to do that you're saying "no" to. Is it that your child wants to use a sharp knife? Or is it that your child climbs all over the furniture in a dangerous way? In either of these cases, you can search for an alternative way for your child to meet their needs. For example, begin having your child practice cutting with a butter knife and a banana. Or, take your child to a jungle gym where climbing is acceptable. By finding outlets that meet our child's needs, we can avoid struggles.

Redirecting

This is the first line of action when your child is doing something they know they're not supposed to do. It is a way to set a firm boundary or limit. Although children often ignore or test the limits we set, this doesn't mean you should remove them. While Montessori advocated following the child and allowing for freedom, she was also very clear about setting limits.

"The liberty of the child ought to have as its limits the collective interest of the community in which he moves; its form is expressed in what we call manners and good behaviour. It is our duty then to protect the child from doing anything which may offend or hurt others, and to check the behaviour which is unbecoming or impolite. But as regards all else, every action

that has a useful purpose, whatever it may be and in whatever forms it shows itself, ought not only to be permitted, but it ought to be kept under observation, that is the essential point."- Maria Montessori, Discovery of the Child

This careful dance between setting limits and permitting freedom is a difficult dance to learn. However, by taking time to carefully observe your child and their actions, you'll learn where to draw the line. Redirecting is one of the most helpful and important techniques that you can use when setting limits.

Redirecting can be a bit of a tricky concept to master, as it is often confused with distracting. However, there are some guidelines for redirecting that can help you use this discipline method correctly.

Redirecting basically involves calling the child back to what they know to do. Using the example from before about my son not taking his dish to the sink, when he forgets to do this, I ask him "Where does your dish belong after eating?" and he immediately remembers. I don't need to scold him, I can simply redirect the behavior from forgetfulness (or laziness!) to being helpful.

This calm way of reminding the child avoids confrontation which can easily alter the mood. In addition, you're assuming that your child has the best intentions. This is a way to respect your child that strengthens your relationship.

Redirecting a behavior can get more complex when it's not a simple task your child forgets to do like putting something away. Here are some examples of how it may work in action for some common behaviors in children ages 2-6:

Getting into Something That's Off Limits

Young children are curious and may try to touch and grab things that are unsafe, meant for adult use only, or simply off limits. Some examples might be a cell phone, a sharp knife or candy. Parents can redirect this behavior by respectfully reminding the child of the expectations and offering an alternative.

The parent might say "I'm sorry, you may not use the phone right now. Would you like to read a book instead?"

Breaking Behavior Rules

You may have some rules in your home about running, how loud your child can be or playing with a ball indoors. When your child breaks the expectations you have laid out, you can redirect them. Here's a great example of something you can say:

"We use a quiet voice indoors. You may go outside if you want to yell."

Basic Guidelines for Redirecting

Redirecting is different than distracting because the behavior isn't ignored. When you redirect behavior, make sure you address what is happening (or not happening) directly, in the most positive way possible. In addition to your attitude, this means your language too. Sometimes there's no other substitute for "no," but where possible, use positive language. For example, instead of "don't run" you can say "walk please," and then state where it's acceptable to run.

Ignoring the behavior can seem attractive especially if you are able to simply distract your child with something else. You may feel like you'll avoid a meltdown or keep your child calmer. But, these short-term gains are long-term losses. Addressing the issue directly helps your child identify exactly what behavior needs to be changed.

The second part of redirecting is helping your child find an appropriate way to behave within the expectations you have set out. It's great if you can offer an alternative that still meets their needs. This is a way of following your child. For example, the child that wanted to use the phone, may be bored and looking for something to do. The child yelling may just enjoy being loud, so offering the opportunity to be loud outside respects their needs.

Children who are as young as 3 can begin to help suggest alternatives. If you feel your child is ready, your redirecting process can include you asking them to help you solve the problem. For example, your child wants to eat candy, but you think they are actually hungry and won't allow them to eat candy at the moment, or perhaps they've even already had some. You can say "I'm sorry, we can't have any candy right now. Maybe you're hungry. Can you think of something else you'd like to eat that's healthier?" Then, help them choose an appropriate snack.

Natural Consequences

Sometimes, the best discipline we can provide is allowing the natural way of things to run its course. Rather than interfering, we can allow our child to feel the natural consequences of their actions.

For example, if your child is playing roughly with a toy, rather than interfere, allow it to break. Your child will learn that by playing roughly, the toys will be ruined.

You can also implement logical consequences for problem behaviors. Traditional discipline often involves enforcing arbitrary punishments that are used across the board for any inappropriate behavior. For example, a child who doesn't clean up their toys may lose technology time or must go to bed early. Logical consequences, in contrast, must be directly related to the behavior. Using the same example, a logical consequence of not cleaning up toys would be to have the toys removed for a few days.

When possible, older children can be involved in the process of deciding what the logical consequence will be. As has been discussed, expectations are key. So, after you've noticed a problem with cleaning up toys and it has been addressed with expectations and redirecting, you can approach your child to discuss the issue. You can say something like "I've noticed you've been having a hard time cleaning up your toys. It's important to me that we keep the house clean. What do you think should happen if you continue to leave your toys out?" You can help your child reach a conclusion that makes sense and is related to the behavior. With this agreement, the next time the expectation about cleaning up toys isn't being met, you must apply the consequence.

Gluing

Montessori said: "Discipline is therefore attained indirectly, that is, by developing activity in spontaneous work."

Basically, this suggests that children who are busily working achieve discipline and are likely to have fewer behavior problems. We must also assume that other needs such as nutrition, sleep and human connection are also being adequately met.

Gluing is a method that can help children find something useful to do by providing a moment to step back and observe. The method is simple. You ask your child to watch what you're doing and then say that you'll find something to do together when you're done. For example: "Come watch me chop these vegetables. Then, we'll find something for us to do together."

It's simple and keeps your child close to you. The idea here is that rather than distancing your child through a time-out, you bring them closer. During this time, your child will observe you doing something useful. If your child asks to join in, you can certainly allow them to help if the task is appropriate. Once you're finished, you can give your child two options for something to do or allow them to think of an activity.

When can you use this technique?

When you have already tried redirecting your child and behavior continues to be an issue, try gluing. Perhaps your child continues to play ball in the house, and this isn't allowed. Or perhaps your child has even become whiny and bored, claiming they have "nothing to do."

This is a way of setting a clear boundary by stopping the unwanted behavior while also providing a solution that respects the child and their need for independence and closeness to you.

A Note on Breaking Things

Spilling, breaking, dropping, these are natural mistakes. While we want to encourage our children to be careful, it's also important that we don't demoralize them.

When it comes to discipline around accidents, there's really no need for much action other than helping the child clean up. Why? Because the mess created from breaking or spilling something is a natural control of error. The consequences of the mistake are clear and obvious. A glass breaks into a thousand shards or cereal is strewn across the floor.

Accidents will happen. Try to be matter of fact and say something like "Oops! The glass broke. I'll help you clean up." Most children don't aim to break and spill things, it's just part of the process of developing motor control. Your child may feel shame or embarrassment over the episode. There's no need to add your criticism on top of this.

Descriptive Praise

One of the best ways you can encourage your child in their good behavior, and help avoid the less pleasant behavior, is through positive reinforcement. In generations past, positive reinforcement has been a wildly popular method for achieving positive behaviors in children. However, it does have some flaws and goes against the Montessori method.

Why?

Traditionally, positive reinforcement uses evaluative praise. This sort of praise often categorizes a child's behavior as "good", or "bad." Some common examples of evaluative praise are "good job", "good girl/boy", "you were awesome!", "beautiful picture!" Each one of these examples shows the adult deciding that the child is "good" or that their work or behavior is "good" rather than "bad."

Evaluative praise was encouraged in the past because in the 1960s and 1970s, researchers showed that children performed better if they had good self-esteem. And one way to increase self-esteem was through praise. Today, researchers have found that excessive use of evaluative praise can have negative effects and even result in narcissism. This is undesirable. So, how can we encourage self-esteem?

Positive self-esteem can also be cultivated through other methods. Montessori believed that children needed to be internally motivated and discouraged the use of external rewards and excessive praise. Yet children still require feedback from their parents, teachers and caregivers.

Descriptive praise is a positive way to encourage your child, cultivate self-esteem and also develop internal motivation in your child.

What is it?

Descriptive praise is very simple. It involves describing the positive things your child is doing and possibly explaining why they're beneficial. For example:

"Thanks for cleaning up the spill. Now the table will be clean for someone else to use"

Or

"I noticed how you were concentrating on drawing that picture. I like the colors you picked."

This is different than evaluative praise that defines whether what your child did was "good" or "bad".

Descriptive praise encourages your child to reflect on what they've done while evaluative praise encourages them to look to others for approval. Children may even feel more empowered with descriptive praise because they learn that they have control over positive outcomes. In the examples given, the adult notices that the child cleaned and made a nice, clean space. The child can easily repeat this action and create a nice, clean space again. Yet if you say "good job!" there's no specific way the child can reproduce this because the praise is dependent on the adult's discretion, which is often arbitrary.

Descriptive praise is a great way to help your child identify their positive behaviors and reflect on why they are good. Focus on aspects of the behavior such as their level of effort, the positive outcomes of their work and how their behavior contributes to the community. These are all things your child has some control over.

I'm reminded of my own child when thinking about descriptive praise that notices effort. We got my 4-year-old a set of markers for his birthday. Especially because they were new, snapping the caps back on the markers was particularly difficult for him. He grew frustrated. My husband encouraged him saying "keep trying, you can do it!" He finally found a method that worked for him. He would press the cap on the table with the marker until he heard the clicking sound that indicated it was on properly. "Wow," my husband said, "look at that. You kept trying and then you did it!" I used this reminder of perseverance often over the next few weeks when he wanted to give up easily. "Remember how you had to keep trying to get the caps on the markers? I bet if you keep trying you'll do it." His eyes would light up remembering, and he would go back to whatever it was he was doing until he achieved his goal.

Descriptive praise provides your child with a helpful commentary on their actions. They can internalize this and over time will begin to recognize the positive aspects of their actions on their own and choose their behaviors accordingly.

The Parent's Role

As parents, we wear many hats. We are teachers, guides, helpers, friends, advocates and most of all, examples. This means that we're being closely watched, every move we make, from our most cheerful moments to our impulsive moments of anger. The following are some tips and tricks to help you as the parent do your best when implementing discipline techniques.

When using any of the techniques described in this chapter, the parent needs to use special care when communicating with their child. Calmness should be a primary goal. Parenting children is very frustrating at times and while it's ok to be angry, it's also in our own best interest to model ideal behaviors for our children. It's impossible to remain calm and collected at all times, which is why it's also ok to tell your child you need a minute. Express your feelings in a way that is clear and simple, "I'm feeling very angry and upset. I'm going to take a break for a minute and then I'll come back to talk."

Next, ensure that your child is in a safe space and go ahead and lock yourself in your bathroom or bedroom. Take a minute to scream, stomp your feet, count to ten, punch a pillow, do whatever it is that you need to do. After you've had a minute, go back and talk with your child about the issue at hand. You'll feel much calmer and you'll be less likely to say or do something you'll later regret.

I have often heard my exact words coming out of my child's mouth. What parent hasn't? That's why it's important to take care what we say. Just as easily as they'll repeat "I love you," they can also repeat "You're driving me crazy!"

Another helpful technique you can use instead of taking a mini-break is to take some deep, belly breaths right there with your child. This technique has been proven to lower your heart beat and stabilize blood pressure, which lowers your anxiety and feelings of stress. In a pinch, just a few deep breaths can be the difference to responding by yelling or responding with respect.

Finally, in your life, ensure that you're taking some time for you. Even 15-20 minutes for a brisk walk or to read a book in peace can be enough to make a difference. Self-care, as it is often called, gives you the energy and inner peace to respond respectfully to your child throughout the day.

If you don't always respond in the most perfect Montessori way, don't worry! Give yourself a break. Parenting is a hard job and the fact that you're trying to do your best is enough. Keep trying and working towards finding the best ways to respond to your child.

Establishing lasting peace is the work of education; all politics can do is keep us out of war.

- DR. MARIA MONTESSORI

CHAPTER FOUR

Handling Conflict

Conflict is part of life. People are social beings, and it's normal for situations of disagreement and conflict to come up in our everyday interactions. Children need help to develop the social skills to deal with conflict. Montessori believed that, just like anything else, we should focus on teaching these skills rather than assuming children will just pick them up.

While using our example and modeling the way to deal with these situations is key, we can give our children other helpful tools for dealing with conflict. This chapter will outline several techniques and tools for teaching children how to handle conflict.

Waiting for a Turn and Sharing

This lesson is important for young children so that they can manage common situations in their daily life. However, we must also recognize the developmental stages children go through. Two-year-olds may still struggle with the concept of taking turns and sharing. It's important to be understanding and not to push things too far with your very young child. Your child may not understand that the item being shared will be given back to them. So, forcing things may not be the best option, especially when the item in question is a favorite, treasured toy.

But, as children grow, they are more socially aware and become able to share. In order to promote sharing and taking turns, some of these lessons can be used:

Sharing Popcorn

This lesson should be given to several children, they could be friends or siblings. Ask the children to sit in a circle. Then, provide a bowl of popcorn (apple slices or another healthy snack also works fine) and one small empty bowl for each child. Demonstrate passing the bowl to the person next to you and offering the child some popcorn. Encourage the child to say "thank you", take some popcorn and then pass the bowl along to the next child.

Waiting for a Turn

The Montessori classroom encourages learning to take a turn by making this a natural part of the environment. There is only one of each material, and children must learn to wait to use the materials if they are being used. This can be a difficult process, but with practice, all children learn to wait for their turn. There is simply no other option.

When children feel frustrated about waiting, parents and teachers should be understanding. After all, don't we get frustrated waiting in long lines for our turn at the bank or post office? It can be very difficult to wait for a long time. Adults also experience time differently than children. Do you remember as a child that 5 minutes felt like an eternity? So, respond to a child who is frustrated about waiting with empathy. Simple phrases like "Yes, it's very hard to wait, isn't it?" validate the child's feelings. You may also consider teaching some coping mechanisms like finding something to do or singing a song while waiting to help the time pass.

You can practice waiting for a turn in everyday life. If you only have one child, consider attending play groups or visiting a local park where other children also play. In situations where other children are around, your child will almost certainly have to wait for their turn at some point.

The Peace Corner

Many primary Montessori classrooms feature a special place called the "peace corner". You can also make one in your home. The purpose of the peace corner is to provide a place for people to be when they are upset, angry, need to take a break or are having a hard time. Usually only one person makes use of the peace corner, but when using it for resolving conflict, two people can use it.

This small space can be unique to you and your family. Here are some guidelines for creating one.

Quiet

The peace corner should be in a quiet place in your home. It could be hidden away so that it is truly a refuge.

What to put in it?

The peace corner should be an inviting, calm space. Here are some commonly found items:

- pillows, cushions, carpet
- a nicely framed photo or drawing that is calming
- something to fiddle with such as a stress ball, mini zen garden, stones for building with, etc.
- a fountain
- a candle
- the peace flower

There is one item that could be considered a requirement for a peace corner, and this is the peace flower. Choose either a silk rose, placed in a vase or use a fresh cut flower in a vase. If you choose to use a real flower, you'll have to make sure it's replaced frequently.

Creating the Peace Corner

Depending on the age of your child, it's a good idea to include them in creating this space. Ask your child to help pick out pillows, choose a picture to display and decide on a calming object to include. Allowing your child to be part of the creation process will give them a sense of ownership and encourage them to use the space.

Presenting the Peace Corner

Choose a time when your child is happy and in a good mood to present the Peace Corner to them. This will ensure that your child understands the idea.

Explain to your child that in life, sometimes we feel sad, angry or upset. Go on to explain that it can be helpful to spend some time alone and take a break when we're feeling this way. Show your child the peace corner and demonstrate how to use any objects you have placed there (mini Zen garden, stress ball, etc.)

Then, tell your child that they can visit the peace corner for a break whenever they'd like.

You may also consider role playing deciding to use the peace corner. You can pretend to be upset, angry or sad. Then say "let's go to the peace corner." Walk over to the corner and sit for a few minutes enjoying the space.

The next time your child is upset, sad or angry, you can invite them to visit the peace corner. For younger children, it's normal that your child may want you to go with them. It's also normal if they emphatically ask you to go away! Try to keep it as a positive option. If they refuse, don't push it. Eventually they may want to try using the peace corner as a safe space when they're having a hard time.

It's also great to model using the peace corner when you're upset or angry. You can say something like "I'm going to take a break in the peace corner," to highlight this choice to your child.

Conflict Resolution Skills

Watching from a distance, I observed how two children were arguing over who would get to use a material first. The two girls were both very insistent. In a very short time, their voices became raised, until one of the girls finally points towards the peace corner. The two walk over together, sit down and go through the conflict resolution ritual until they reach an agreement. They hug and move on. It's beautiful.

Just days earlier, the other teachers and I had demonstrated how to use the peace corner for dealing with a disagreement. We had acted out a similar scenario, pretending we were fighting over who would get to use a material first. The children watched in shock at our argument. It made the next steps all the more memorable, showing them how to communicate with each other when strong feelings are at play.

Conflict resolution skills can be taught first by using the peace corner and the peace flower. I also want to note that while 3-year-olds can benefit from observing the use of the peace flower in action, they may not be ready to actually do it until they are a bit older. Use your judgement when deciding when to introduce this concept to your child. Once children become good at these skills, they can practice them without the help of the flower or peace corner.

How does it work? Ideally you and another adult can demonstrate the conflict resolution skills you're hoping to develop in your child:

1. Act out a conflict. It's often easy for children at this age to understand fighting over an object, and not wanting to share. It makes the conflict easy to identify and relatable.

2. One of the adults should suggest going to the peace corner. The other agrees.

3. They sit down. One of the adults holds the peace flower close to their heart and says an "I feel" statement. For example, "I feel upset because you grabbed the ball I wanted to play with."

4. Then, the person who spoke passes the flower to the other person. The second person responds with an "I feel" statement. For example, "I'm also upset because I wanted to play with the ball and you never let me use it."

5. The adults continue passing the flower back and forth and talking. Eventually they reach an agreement such as taking turns, playing together, putting the ball away and playing with something else, finding a second ball, etc.

6. Finally, one of the adults explains that the role play is over and emphasizes that whoever is holding the peace flower is the only one who can talk. The other person waits their turn. Explain that the flower is used because it is delicate and easily damaged, just like our feelings. For this reason, we must be careful with the flower and each other's feelings.

7. Then invite the child or children to use the space and flower for handling arguments whenever they'd like.

This method works really well for groups of children and classrooms. Within the home, it can be very useful for helping siblings learn to get along. However, you may not have the chance to share these skills with other children with whom your child interacts. As your child grows, you may consider role-playing how they might lead in a conflict situation with another child who has never used the peace flower or peace corner.

Independence and Conflict Resolution

I cringed while watching my son playing with his cousins. The play fighting was clearly not so playful anymore. However, I fought the urge to step in and "make peace." By allowing him and his cousins to handle the situation and find resolution allowed them to practice problem-solving skills and work on their social interactions. In the end, no one was severely injured, the older children comforted the younger ones and they continued playing. I didn't even lift a finger!

Children have their own ways of resolving conflict. While we adults would often like to see them apologize, talk about their feelings and hug at the end, these are skills that come over time and may not accurately reflect the child's style or relationships. If we constantly interrupt and intervene in conflicts, we'll never give them the chance to learn to solve their own problems and deal with conflict.

While teaching about conflict resolution and role-playing are positive ways to help our children learn these skills, intervening is often a way that we show our children that we don't trust them to handle things. This is not to say that parents should never intervene. Cases where children may be injured or experience serious emotional damage require our intervention. However, the majority of the time, we can trust our children to handle their own conflicts.

Our role is to provide support and guidance when our children ask for it. This may mean comforting your child when things don't go their way or when they get hurt. It also means talking through tough situations they've experienced and coming up with creative ways they could deal with things in the future, and then trusting them to do so.

Independence in conflict resolution can seem like a tricky balance to handle. We as parents must often make a hard choice to watch longer than what's comfortable and step in only when it's really necessary. While each parent will decide this for themselves, I encourage you to re-evaluate your boundaries.

Here are some helpful questions to ask before stepping in:

- Are you stepping in because you're too uncomfortable or because your child is?

- Has your child come to you for help? It's likely they will if you're watching and they truly feel worried. Even if they do come to you, you may consider helping them think of a strategy they can try on their own and allowing them to put it into action independently.

- Is anyone in danger of being seriously injured (more than a scratch or a bump)?

- Are the children no longer enjoying the game? If so, does it appear that they're trying to work through this (arguing, talking, choosing sides)?

- Finally, make yourself wait a few more minutes if no one is in danger of being hurt. You may be surprised to see that they resolve the issue on their own, without your help.

In the case that you do intervene, instead of taking over, try asking questions to help the children find their way through the conflict. You may ask "What are you playing?" or "It looks like you're having a hard time getting along. What might you change to make this game fun for everyone?" Often, the simple presence of an adult can cause a change in dynamics (also the very reason it's important to carefully consider intervention) and give the children a pause in which they redesign their play, making it more fun and light-hearted again.

"We must help the child to act for himself, will for himself, think for himself; this is the art of those who aspire to serve the spirit."
- DR. MARIA MONTESSORI

CHAPTER FIVE

Feeling and Expressing Big Emotions

Temper tantrums, lashing out, hitting, biting and screaming are all examples of how children may express big feelings. Whether the root cause is anger, sadness or fear, children make it clear that something is wrong.

In my first year of teaching, there were some very expressive children at the school. I will never forget the day I heard yelling from one of the smaller classrooms. Wondering what was going on, I poked my head in to see a child just tipping over the trashcan on top of his teacher's head! In shock, I asked the child to come outside with me for a break. He ended up crying and was upset for a while longer. Eventually he came around and decided to apologize to the teacher.

There's a careful balance when it comes to emotions. It's important for children to express themselves, even when their emotions are strong and ugly. Repressing or bottling up these emotions is not healthy. When we ask children to "stop crying" or tell them "it's ok," or try to calm them down before they're ready, is communicating to them that those emotions aren't ok or acceptable. This can be very confusing for children because when they're happy, we accept this emotion and embrace it.

Expecting our children to be happy all the time is unreasonable. We as adults don't feel happy all of the time. Life is full of lots of emotions. Some are difficult. So, to help our children express themselves, we need to provide excellent examples and teach coping strategies.

Montessori often spoke about serving the spirit and respect:

"Children are human beings to whom respect is due, superior to us by reason of their innocence and of the greater possibilities of their future."

As our children are expressing their very big, sometimes ugly feelings, we must hold these words in our hearts. It can be very helpful to recognize our own feelings when observing our children. A very angry child can bring up our own uncomfortable feelings and cause us to react strongly. Yet, if we accept that we are feeling uncomfortable when faced with this strong display of anger because perhaps we often suppress our own feelings of anger, we can become more open to accepting our child's anger.

One of the greatest ways we can show respect to our children is by empathizing with them. By showing our children empathy and trying to put ourselves in their shoes, we take the first steps towards interacting with them respectfully and lovingly.

In this chapter, techniques and coping mechanisms will be shared so that you can help your child learn to express their emotions in a healthy way. In addition, behavioral problems such as tantrums, hitting and biting, that are usually a result of not having an outlet for emotions, will be discussed.

Tantrums

The age of 2 and 3 are infamous for being difficult years for parents. Mainstream culture has even given each year their own special name: "The terrible twos" and "threenagers." Although children are curious and learn a lot around this age, it is also an age where frustration is still commonplace and children haven't necessarily learned coping mechanisms for their anger, frustration or even sadness.

Even those who follow the Montessori philosophy may find themselves facing a very expressive child who chooses tantrums as the main form of communication when they are angry, sad or frustrated. I have been on the receiving end of many a tantrum. However, with patience, love and some helpful techniques, these bursts of emotion become less common and more tempered.

Before continuing, I would also like to say that tantrums are normal. They are even healthy. Some researchers assert that tantrums are a natural way for young children to release stress. This is in line with what many psychologists and parenting experts believe. So, whether we like it or not, as parents, we must prepare ourselves to deal with tantrums because they are part of parenting.

When it comes to tantrums, parents can often feel them coming. This is because tantrums are often a way of expressing a need such as a need to sleep, hunger, or frustration. We see that the storm is brewing and will reach the boiling point any minute. No matter how hard we fight against it, a child who is ready for a tantrum lets it out sooner or later.

Other times, tantrums are a direct response to an upsetting situation. Perhaps you tell your child it's time to leave the park. Or maybe they don't like what's been offered for lunch. Sometimes a tantrum can result from asking your child to complete a simple task such as picking up toys or hanging up a jacket. In these cases, you can help by preparing your child. For example, give your child a few minutes warning before changing activities. Or, give your child a choice when cleaning up such as, "Do you want to pick up the blocks or put away your clothes first?" Even if you still end up with a tantrum, offering choices and alerting your child of changes can help them feel a bit more in control. Eventually, the tantrums come less frequently and intensely.

In other cases, tantrums can be a way of expressing pent-up emotion from a previous frustration or upset. These tantrums are not as easy to predict, and often appear when we think everything has been going well. Then, your child suddenly notices that the wheels on her car don't turn just so, or that his cookie is broken and bursts into tears. These tantrums may show up while you're having a particularly good day because your child feels exceptionally safe, so safe that they can express the worst feelings they have.

Addressing Tantrums

When you're at home, tantrums can be allowed to run their course. Hand in Hand Parenting recommends using a technique known as "stay listening." While many researchers suggest that doing nothing during a tantrum is the best course of action, Hand in Hand Parenting offers a nuance that is much more respectful of the child and their needs. Rather than leaving your child alone in their tantrum, you can say something like "I'm sorry you're feeling so bad. I'm here with you, and whenever you're ready I'll be ready to give you a hug." Meanwhile, you can continue to go about whatever you're doing. This statement and staying close-by and accessible to your child shows your support, rather than ignoring or essentially disapproving of this show of emotion.

Notice that the feelings are validated and named in this technique. Use variations as you see appropriate, for example "You seem frustrated" or "I see that you're angry I won't let you buy the toy." By naming the frustration, you help your child identify what's going on and why they're feeling the way they are. Young children may still have a hard time naming feelings and understanding what instigates them. Use a matter of fact tone when naming what you observe and then highlight your presence and openness to comfort them when they're ready.

If you're in public, tantrums present a different level of difficulty. Many a time, I've scooped up my little one and continued walking or made my way home, while he kicked and screamed the whole way. This is important and difficult work. It's tempting to buy a lollipop or toy, or appease our child in any way possible to make it through the outing without making a scene. Yet, this doesn't address the true cause of the upset and rather teaches our children that through crying and fussing, they'll get a treat.

Rather, acknowledge your child's feelings as in "stay listening" and try to get to a safe or acceptable place for the tantrum to pass. If you're at the grocery store or shopping, the car can be a safe option, or simply outside where you won't attract as much attention. If the tantrum seems to have started off because of hunger or tiredness, try to find a way to meet these needs.

After the Tantrum

Once a tantrum is over, it's helpful to spend some quality time with your child connecting in a positive way. Read a book together, play a game or do something that your child enjoys together. By re-connecting, you help your child feel safe and calm again.

Hitting and Biting

Hitting and biting are frightening for parents. We wonder where our little ones learned it and why they are behaving this way. We may even feel embarrassed about it and wonder what other parents will say.

The truth is that many children go through a stage of hitting and biting when they are very young. Most outgrow it by around the age of two. But, for some children, it continues past toddlerhood, or even begins a bit later when the child is 3 or 4. In these cases, the child is often experiencing a great frustration or anger and has chosen to hit or bite to express these feelings.

Young children may feel anger and frustration when they are unable to express themselves because language is still new to them. They may also be scared and anxious about a big change happening in their lives such as the birth of a sibling or beginning school. Hitting and biting can also simply be a response to specific situations where your child may feel threatened or angry.

The good news is that children almost always grow out of hitting and biting. How many adults do you know that hit and bite? However, children don't grow out of feelings. We need to help them express these feelings in other, more healthy ways that don't harm others.

So, what can you do if your child hits and bites?

Safety First

If your child's hitting and biting is directed at you, keep yourself safe. Hold them off at arm's length or catch their hand before it strikes you. Let your child know what you're doing. For example, say, "I won't let you hurt me. My safety is important."

If your child is hitting and biting others, you'll have to be on even higher alert and intervene when you see your child ready to strike or bite another child or adult. You can use the same methods.

State Feelings

Similarly to during a tantrum, it's important to say the emotions you see that your child may be experiencing. Also note the circumstances as appropriate. For example, "I see you're angry that Bryan won't give you the toy."

Play or Cry

I've had success turning a situation of hitting into play. My son enjoys rough housing (as do many little ones) and sometimes when I deflect his hitting, I give him a big smile and playfully bat at him as well. Or, I get a big, scared look on my face and act out an exaggerated fall as he pushes me. This gives him a sense of power and allows him to relax and play, rather than fighting.

This certainly isn't acceptable in all situations, but by reading your child, you can decide whether or not to try it. I find this sort of playing very helpful in diffusing tension for some situations. As parents, we often say "no" and set boundaries more than we think in a day. This is good. But, it also means our little ones can feel defeated. This sort of playing often works for me when my son asks for something that I say "no" to, and he may already be feeling tired and frustrated. So, setting that last boundary pushes him over the edge and he lashes out. I respond by playing and being "weak", which is hilarious for him. Laughter can often serve the same purpose as crying when releasing tensions.

On the other hand, children who are hitting and biting may release the tension by crying. As you thwart their efforts to harm others, they grow more and more upset until they cry and throw a tantrum. Or, they may become standoffish and want to be alone. Here, you can follow the same steps as when handling a tantrum. Express your support and willingness to talk and comfort them once they've calmed down.

Helpful Techniques for Expressing Emotions

In a more peaceful moment, you can practice helping your child to express themselves appropriately. There are many options that you can use, depending on your child's preferences and temperament.

Choose a moment to teach these techniques when your child is happy and cooperative. Explain that you're going to pretend being angry or frustrated. Then, choose a technique to teach your child. Here are some easy to teach options:

1. Take deep breaths.
2. Hit pillows or have a pillow fight.
3. Stomp feet.
4. Break sticks
5. Play drums
6. Use the peace corner

It's best to teach only one of these at a time. Teach the one you'd like to show your child, and demonstrate it. I find it useful to make angry faces just before, to really enact the situation and then say "I'm feeling angry," and then demonstrate the technique. When finished demonstrating you can say "I feel much better," and then ask your child to try.

When your child is about to have a tantrum, or has been hitting or biting, then you can invite your child to use the technique you've practiced. You can slowly build, teaching your child new techniques so that they can choose from the options you give them.

At first, your child may not want to use any of the coping mechanisms when they really need to. Keep offering it as an option and practicing or role-playing when your child is happy, and eventually they will probably choose to use it. These coping mechanisms will give your child healthy outlets that are safe for everyone involved.

For older children, you may also want to discuss what coping mechanisms they suggest or prefer. This was effective for me when dealing with a very angry child. Every day after outdoor playtime at school, a 6-year-old boy completely lost it when asked to come indoors. We tried to warn him a few minutes before outdoor time would end with no success. So, finally, I decided to ask him how we could avoid the daily meltdown. We spent a few minutes discussing his frustrations. I suggested a few ideas and we talked through a few of his. We finally agreed that when outdoor time was over, he would walk through our school's peace maze two times before coming inside. The peace maze was in a swirl shape, and involved walking in a spiral towards the center, and then back out again. It was a very small maze and only took about a minute to walk to the center and out again. Yet, it was a meditative activity that helped calm his spirit before coming inside again.

Whining

"I want the book noooooowww!" "I don't waaanna work right now" "I'm hungry!" What parent hasn't heard a whiny voice speaking these words, or something similar.

Yet, at the same time, what parent hasn't felt similar emotion to that being expressed by our little ones? Perhaps your boss asks you to complete a task that feels unfair or annoying that makes you feel like whining. Or maybe you actually do whine, although probably not directly to your boss, but to an empathetic colleague or your spouse.

Whining often comes as a result of feeling that things are out of your control. For children, it's the same. So, the first step is to respond the way you would to a colleague who wants to vent to you. You can say "Oh, yes that's frustrating that you want the book." You may even join with your child in whining, and express the same sentiments right alongside them. For example, "We don't feel like cleaning, no no no no no!"

Then, you can offer a suggestion for a better way for your child to express themselves. When they're asking for something in a whiny voice, you can say "Did you mean to say, 'Can you help me get a snack please?'" By modeling and demonstrating the way we expect our child to ask for things, we help them find ways to voice their needs respect-fully.

I've gone through this routine so often with my son, all it takes now is for me to look confused and ask "What?" when he asks for something in a whiny voice. He immediately reverts and asks "Can you help me please?" with a much more pleasant tone of voice.

If you're having particular trouble with a whiny child, you can al-ways try talking about it when your child is in a more cooperative, peaceful mood. Role playing is fun for young children and they'll have a laugh if you play whine to them about something. Then, they can play the role of the parent and demonstrate the better way to com-municate the need or feeling.

CHAPTER SIX

Conclusion

One of our greatest responsibilities as parents is to guide our children's character development. As Montessori so aptly says,

"Character formation cannot be taught. It comes from experience and not from explanation."

The experiences our children have, including how we use discipline, the expectations we lay out and how we respond to them in their best and worst moments, shape them for the rest of their lives. Using the Montessori philosophy as a guide for our parenting makes respect, connection and following the child the center of our focus. The techniques that have been outlined in this book allow for you to create a close, meaningful relationship with your child while still giving them the boundaries and limits they need.

Montessori's philosophy also highlights teaching behaviors that we expect to see in our children through positive experiences and demonstrations. Rather than lecturing and punitive punishments, Montessori encourages us to seek to understand our children by observing them carefully so that we can identify their needs. This way, whether they need to express a hurt, an opportunity to practice sharing or the confidence to ask a new friend to play, we can provide them with support and help meet these needs.

Throughout the parenting journey, patience is also an overwhelming theme. While I would love to report that I've been able to solve every discipline problem and difficult behavior I've encountered as a teacher and mother with a few easy steps, this simply isn't the reality. Patience is the key ingredient towards reaching every child and finding a way to help them become peaceful, productive and happy. Persistence is also necessary on our part. And while it's important to be consistent, sometimes what seems to be the obvious solution for dealing with a situation, actually backfires and we have to try something else. Remember that first and foremost, Montessori urges us to follow our children, and this may mean that sometimes we must change course.

As you continue on your parenting journey, I encourage you to embrace following your child and be patient with yourself. If you find yourself overwhelmed, try picking just one new technique to implement or lesson to teach in a week. After a few weeks, you'll be amazed at the progress you're making.

Finally, remember to be generous to yourself in the same way that you are generous to your child. Parenting is a difficult job! Try as we may to do things "perfectly," sometimes we mess up. It's ok to apologize to our children, and forgive ourselves. Even in this, we are providing a valuable example to our children about how to be human.

I wish you the best of luck on your parenting journey and hope that your days are filled with joy as you watch your little ones grow and change!

Addressing Difficult Topics

Some of life's realities are not always easy to explain to kids. It may be because we're uncomfortable with the topics ourselves, or because their reactions are difficult for us to handle.

I'll never forget when my almost 4-year-old realized that death was final, not only for animals, but for people too. "But Mama," he sobbed, "If I die, how will I get up?" My heart broke in two trying to explain to him that eventually, our bodies just stop working. I comforted and hugged him, but this harsh reality was difficult for him to take in.

So, how to handle these topics? Age appropriate honesty is the best place to start, but even then, it's sometimes hard to know what to say or how to handle our children's questions. Here are some suggestions for how to handle some of the more difficult topics we must tackle as parents.

Death

Depending on you and your family's beliefs, you can handle this topic accordingly. What's suggested here doesn't reflect any religion, but the information can be helpful when talking to your child about death.

This topic inevitably comes up naturally. Perhaps a relative passes away. Or maybe a pet dies. Even when a child stomps on an ant, the topic of death can come up. Because Montessori encouraged respect and love for all living things, you can use insects and animals as an opportunity to talk about how special and beautiful life is.

Whenever you're in the outdoors with your child, you can take the time to notice insects and animals. If your child feels an urge to step on them or kill them, explain that the insect isn't bothering them and it's not very kind to kill it. These sorts of experiences with death can help your child begin to understand what death means.
Older children may also study the lifecycle of a plant or animal. You can include death as a part of the lifecycle as well.

Books and movies are other places your child may be exposed to the idea of death. At any of these times when your child comes in contact with death, try to talk about it as naturally as possible. Answer your child's questions honestly. Here are some common questions children have and suggested answers:

Why do people/animals die? Our bodies can't live forever. Eventually they stop working if we get too sick or if we get hurt really badly.

Will I die? Yes. You'll probably live a very long time and enjoy a wonderful life. But, everyone dies sometime.

What happens when people die? Answer this question according to your beliefs. With older children, you may also want to share what other people believe, ie "Some people believe in reincarnation which means that after people die, they are born again as an animal or another person."

Sex

Another difficult topic to address. Most parents want their children to be informed about sex, but may struggle with talking about it. Other parents struggle with the age of their children and aren't sure when it's ok to talk about it.

This is all much easier when sex is introduced early on in a natural, normal way. Having the "big talk" makes sex seem like something big and scary. It also separates it from everyday life when really, sex and sexuality *is* a part of our lives on a daily basis.

I admit, I struggled with this at first, but after I forced some of it out, it started to feel more normal. Now, I don't worry about it at all! So, how do you talk about sex in a progressive way that's age-appropriate for your child?

1. **Start with body parts**.

   As your two-year-old is in the bath, name the parts of their body while bathing. Use normal body-part names, not nicknames. So, for a boy you could say, "wash your arms, your tummy, your penis and bottom." For a girl, you can use "vulva" as this best expresses the outer genitals that are visible to your daughter. Because she views this area as principly for peeing at this point, it's best to say "vulva" rather than "vagina" because "vagina" would focus only on the sexual function. "Vulva" is more inclusive of all the functions of her genitals.

2. **Acknowledge differences.**

   Especially if nudity is normal in your family, your children will start to notice differences in body parts between males and females. Nudity as normal within the family can actually be helpful, sex therapist Dr. Dennis Sugrue says. Researchers have learned that children who grew up in homes where nudity was normal are more likely to grow up feeling comfortable with and accepting of their bodies and sexuality.

If you're not comfortable with nudity or if there aren't members of both sexes in your home, consider getting a book that shows the differences between girls' and boys' bodies. If your family does practice nudity as normal within the home, your child may naturally notice and ask about differences between their body and their parent's bodies or between two members of your family's bodies. Just answer in a matter-of-fact, but honest way. For most young children, knowing the names of body parts and knowing which parts belong to a boy or girl is enough to quench their curiosity.

3. Where do babies come from?

By the time your child reaches the age of 3 or 4, you can explain that a baby is made by a woman and a man together and that a baby grows in the uterus of its mama.

4. Privacy

Around the same time (3 or 4) you can also begin explaining where it's acceptable to be naked, and where it's not. For example, it's ok to be naked at home, but not in public. Children should also begin to understand that no one should touch their genitals other than themselves, a parent or a doctor.

The more open and honest you are about sex and sexuality, the more likely your child will see it as normal and good. By starting the conversation early, you'll set a precedent that it's ok to talk about these topics, meaning your child will be more likely to consult you with questions in the future.

If your child brings up these topics at inappropriate times or places you can always use redirecting techniques. Other children may begin to find potty humor quite entertaining. This is a normal phase. Simply set boundaries as necessary about where and when it's ok to use this humor and enjoy the laughs. They'll get over it eventually.

Talking openly about sex and sexuality is important for your child's health and safety. While some parents may find it a bit uncomfortable to begin discussing these topics with their children, the alternative of them learning from other kids at school or from what society shows them isn't ideal. There are many resources available online or through family organizations to provide you further direction when addressing this topic with your child. Make use of them and when in doubt, be honest and matter of fact.

Strangers and Dangers

While we want to keep our children safe, we may struggle with how to warn our children of dangers without causing excessive fear. Conversations about strangers, sexual abuse and even guns are necessary topics to cover, but may be tricky to bring up. By staying matter of fact and using age appropriate information, you can ensure that your child knows enough to be safe without traumatizing them. Here are some pointers for touching on these topics:

Strangers

Explain to your child that while most people in the world are good, there may be some people who wish to hurt them. Tell your child that because of this, you need them to follow some rules. Some good guidelines to start with are that:

- A parent must always know where you are.
- Only accept food and candy from close friends and family.
- If you ever feel uncomfortable with anyone, tell your parents or someone you trust.

Sexual Abuse

As stated in the previous section, it's wise to tell your child that no one should touch their genitals except for parents and doctors. It's also necessary to go further to explain that some people may ask them to touch their private parts, and that this is also not ok. Because sexual abuse perpetrators are often known to the victim, you must stress that if anyone wants them to do anything involving their private parts, they must tell you right away. You may also consider giving your child some clear actions in case they find themselves in a situation of abuse such as screaming, saying "no" very loudly or calling for help. Keep the conversation simple and straight forward. Explain to your child that it's not likely to happen, but you just want to be sure they're safe.

Guns

Whether or not you have a gun in your home, a close friend of your child may have a gun in their home. By informing your child about guns, what they look like and what they do, you can save your child from a potentially dangerous situation. Tell your child if they ever see a gun not to touch it, even if a friend says it's a toy. Ask your child to tell you right away if they see a gun. It's also wise as parents to ask your child's friend's parents if they keep a gun at home before allowing a play date or visit. Unfortunately, even if families keep guns hidden, children may find them and the consequences are very serious.

How to Introduce Montessori When You Didn't Begin at Birth

While it would be great if all parents could know about Montessori from the start, the reality is that not all of us do. If you've discovered Montessori and want to begin implementing it, but have used different parenting techniques in the past, you may feel like you don't know quite how to get started. It's normal to feel overwhelmed by all that there is to learn, and also to feel a bit confused about how to begin implementing the philosophy with your child.

Here are some tips for getting started with Montessori with your older child:

1. **Read**.

   Inform yourself as much as you can about the Montessori philosophy. Many helpful guides and books have been written about Montessori that can give you an overview of her philosophy and her life. It's often easiest to read about the philosophy and gain an understanding of the basic ideas and then delve into some of Montessori's original writings. Montessori's writings are full of wisdom and insights on children. However, they are also a bit complex, and academic in nature, making for a difficult read if you don't already have the overall grasp of the philosophy. But, after you've taken the time to get to know the philosophy, you'll truly appreciate Montessori's amazing analysis of the child, childhood development and how they learn. *The Absorbent Mind* is a great book of Montessori's to start with.

2. **Take it one step at a time.**

There are a lot of small steps you can take to begin implementing the Montessori philosophy in your home and in your parenting. Try to pick one small thing to try each week and work on it with your child. You may begin by taking a week to make each room in your home child-friendly. Or, it can be as simple as encouraging your child's independence by showing your child taking their dish to the sink or hang up their jacket up each day after school. Then, the next week, practice your descriptive praise and try to give your child one form of descriptive praise every day. Over time, you'll incorporate more and more of the philosophy into your parenting, until you can confidently call yourself a "Montessori parent."

3. **Explain to your child.**

If some parts of the Montessori philosophy are quite different from the way you used to do things, tell your child. For example, if you used to put your child in time out, you might say "We're not going to do time out anymore. Instead, we're going to spend more time together while still making sure we follow the rules." Then, you can implement redirecting and gluing instead.

4. **Expect it to take time.**

It can take some time for you and your child to adapt to the philosophy. It would be wonderful if implementing the philosophy instantly produced positive changes in your relationship to your child and your child's behavior. But, these things take time. After all, your child must grow accustomed to the new way of doing things, and so must you.

5. **Be consistent.**

In this book, I've encouraged following the child and adjusting your approach with your child as needed. But, especially when starting out, be consistent with what you're doing for a few weeks before you change your approach. This will give you and your child time to adjust to the new way of doing things.

6. **Find support.**

Finally, and most importantly, find an interactive Montessori resource to guide you as you begin. Whether you join an online forum of parents who practice Montessori, take an online course or find a fellow Montessori parent nearby in your community whom you can talk to and enjoy playdates with, you'll benefit greatly from the support. It's often so helpful to talk over different experiences you may have with your child or discuss how well some strategies may fit in with the philosophy. A more seasoned Montessorian may be able to provide wonderful insight to struggles you'll go through with your child or simply affirm your efforts.

Resources

www.montessori.org

(2017). Retrieved 3 February 2017, from http://www.montessori.org.uk/magazine-and-jobs/library_and_study_resources/teacher-training-study-resources/topics/rewards_and_punishments

Center, N. & Center, N. (2017). Redirecting Versus Distracting in the Montessori Environment. Montessoritraining.blogspot.com. Retrieved 3 February 2017, from http://montessoritraining.blogspot.com/2014/11/redirecting-versus-distracting-montessori.html

Discipline — The Montessori Center. (2017). Montessoricenterbend.com. Retrieved 3 February 2017, from http://www.montessoricenterbend.com/discipline/

Early Language Development Articles – Helpful Information and Tips for Parents. (2017). *Hanen.org.* Retrieved 3 February 2017, from http://www.hanen.org/Helpful-Info/Professional-Articles/The-Power-or-Perils-of-Praise--Revisiting-assumpti.aspx

Hand in Hand - Supporting Parents for 25 Years. Today It's Your Turn. (2017). Hand in Hand Parenting. Retrieved 3 February 2017, from http://www.handinhandparenting.org/

Irinyi, M. (2017). Montessori Parenting: Logical and Natural Consequences. Montessoritraining.blogspot.com. Retrieved 3 February

2017, from http://montessoritraining.blogspot.com/2009/07/montessori-parenting-logical-and.html

Montessori Toddlers Who Are Not Yet Peaceful: Dealing With a Tantrum the Montessori Way. (2017). Montessoritraining.blogspot.com. Retrieved 3 February 2017, from http://montessoritraining.blogspot.com/2010/10/montessori-insights-and-reflections-of_07.html

Montessori, M. (1967). The absorbent mind (1st ed.). New York: Holt, Rinehart and Winston.

"The Naked Truth On Family Nudity". Parents. N.p., 2016. Web. 30 Sept. 2016.

Three Keys to Transforming Whining. (2017). Awake Parent. Retrieved 3 February 2017, from http://www.awakeparent.com/Shelly/transforming-whining/

Understanding Tears and Tantrums. (2017). Awareparenting.com. Retrieved 3 February 2017, from http://www.awareparenting.com/tantrums.htm

About the Author

Rachel Peachey is a Montessori teacher, freelance writer and mom of two little ones. She enjoys living in beautiful Guatemala with her husband and children who were born in 2013 and 2015. She devotes her free time to homeschooling her kids and running a community library she began in 2016 at the local Catholic church.

Visit her website and blog: www.rachelpeachey.com

About the Publishers

Ashley and Mitchell Sterling are new author/indie-publishers and video-bloggers on YouTube known as 'Fly by Family'. When they're not writing or talking to a camera lens, the Sterlings value their time together, in the beautiful bluegrass-laden wilderness of eastern Kentucky, where they live with their two children, Nova and Mars.

-Visit their website: www.sterlingproduction.com
-Visit them on YouTube: www.youtube.com/flybyfamily

Thank you for reading our book! We would love to hear from you in an honest review on Amazon or Goodreads!
Sincerely,
Ashley and Mitchell Sterling

97470050R00044

Made in the USA
Middletown, DE
05 November 2018